HOW TO
SMALL
BIBLE S

C000217312

A Guide to Discussion Study

Revised Edition

Marilyn Kunz and
Catherine Schell

small group bible studies

Marshalls

Marshalls Paperbacks
Marshall Morgan & Scott
3 Beggarwood Lane, Basingstoke, Hants, RG23 7LP, UK

British Library CIP data
Schell, Catherine
   How to start a small group Bible study.——
   (Small group Bible studies)
   1. Bible——Study   2. Small groups
   I. Title   II. Kunz, Marilyn   III. Series
   220'.7   BS600.2

   ISBN 0 – 551 – 01237 – 4

Printed in Great Britain by Stanley L. Hunt (Printers) Ltd. Rushden,
Northamptonshire.

Contents

IF you would like to start a discussion Bible study with your neighbors, friends at work, or people you know through community contacts, here is how to begin . . .

FIRST, make sure you build bridges of friendship with the people you intend to invite. They should know you well enough to believe that you will not embarrass them.

NEXT, pray that God will give your friends a desire to study the Bible.

THEN, invite them to come to your home or the home of someone who is starting the group with you. For a lunch-hour group at work, find a conference room or office in which to meet together.

BE SURE TO make it clear that people are invited to come and to HEAR ABOUT the idea of a discussion Bible study group for adults who are new to Bible study. Do not invite them to "join," but to come "to hear about."

PRESENT the ideas on pages 4-15 of this booklet and have a brief sample discussion on Mark 2:1-12 as described on pages 11-13. Follow the suggestions on pages 14 and 15, and so your group begins!

IN PRESENTING THE IDEA OF SMALL GROUP BIBLE STUDIES STRESS THESE POINTS:

1. This group is NOT for experts.

2. To be in a small group Bible study a person need only believe that the Bible is worth studying.

3. This group is for those who don't know much about the Bible but who would like to discover for themselves what the Bible says.

4. It will not be a lecture series, but a series of informal discussions.

5. Everyone will take a turn leading the discussion with the aid of a study guide which supplies questions to help the group study the chapter carefully. The leader is the question-asker for the session.

6. The person who leads the group by asking the questions often learns the most. Taking weekly turns being question-asker means that each person develops skills in leadership. No one is forced to take a turn, but most people find that they enjoy it. It is only fair to share the maximum learning experience which this provides.

7. People learn as they express their discoveries. One person's insights sharpen another's understanding. Participation in the discussion increases. Interest grows.

8. It is healthy for a group to have people from different backgrounds to share ideas as the group learns together.

9. Most groups meet weekly for about an hour and a half. Some groups at work meet twice a week at lunch for 30-40 minutes. Evening groups often meet for short series of six to eight weeks.

EXPLAIN THE RULES
FOR A GOOD DISCUSSION:

1. Stay with the chapter under consideration. Do not refer to or discuss other portions in the Bible. Learn everything you can from *this* chapter. This will help everyone not to be confused. (Most of us are beginners at studying the Bible as adults.) In addition, references to other portions of the Bible may not be to the point.

2. As a group goes on, members may refer back to the portions they have studied together. They build a common frame of reference for discussion.

3. Get a thorough grasp of the Gospel of Mark as a foundation to which the rest of the Bible can be added and related later.

4. Avoid tangents which frequently become the exchange of mutual ignorance. If a digression occurs, say: "Do we find the answer to that problem here?" or, "What does this paragraph seem to emphasize?" or, "Let's finish the chapter and then those who want to discuss that issue can stay and do so."

5. Allow the Bible portion to speak for itself. Try to discover together what the author is saying. Avoid quoting other authorities: "My pastor says . . ." or "The Reader's Digest said . . ." or "I read somewhere . . ." or "I saw a film. . . ." The Bible is the authority for your study.

6. Encourage all to take part, but don't embarrass anyone by calling his or her name and then asking a question. Ask a question; give everyone a chance to think. Then, if no one answers, call on someone who looks as if he has an answer. After he speaks say, "What do the rest of you think?" (This applies to thought questions, not to simple questions of fact.) In most cases, several people in the group respond to the question, each adding a slightly different dimension.

EMPHASIZE:

Although the leader guides the group, everyone participates and people are free to say: "I don't understand this."

"I don't agree with you."

"This is something I've always wondered about."

Avoid technical expressions not found in the chapter you are discussing. For example, the terms "born again" and "saved" are not found in Mark 2, but "your sins are forgiven" is there.

Studying together is better than studying alone because everyone gets to see the chapter from different viewpoints, through several minds instead of only one. We help one another to discover what the Bible actually says and what it means. We can share together how it applies to our own lives.

RECOMMEND:

The rotation of meeting place in different homes. The discussion leader and the host(ess) should not be the same person at any given meeting. The leader should not have to be concerned with answering the telephone or serving coffee.

Meeting in different homes helps all involved to realize that the Bible study belongs to them and it does not become "the Smith's Bible study." Also, people have opportunity to discuss spiritual issues in their own home where they discuss everything else vital to them and their family.

Coffee and doughnuts or the equivalents are good companions for discussion. Eat *while* you discuss. This saves time, and people are more relaxed.

Time is important. Don't waste it. Promptness is a courtesy. The leader for the day should begin and close the discussion on time. Allow an hour and fifteen minutes for the actual study. Another quarter hour is quickly spent in arrival and farewells.

RECOMMENDED TOOLS FOR A SMALL GROUP BIBLE STUDY:

1. Various recent translations of the Bible will help to broaden your understanding of what it says. Everyone brings whatever translation he has, or buys a contemporary translation.

2. A good English dictionary is helpful to look up words for precise definitions.

3. Study guides will save the leader much time and labor in formulating questions for group discussion. Available guides are listed on page 24. Each person should have his or her own copy of the study guide to use in preparation for the discussion. The discussion will run more smoothly if everyone has a guide to refer to.

Mark: Examine the Record is the study guide of the Gospel of Mark, the first unit of study.

4. Commentaries should not be used for the first few weeks. Then, if you do use a commentary be sure to study the chapter first on your own. Otherwise you will be able to see only what the commentator says. Never take a commentary to the discussion because it, rather than the Bible, will tend to become the authority for the group.

NOW after outlining all these ideas and recommendations of Small Group Bible Studies, lead a brief sample study . . .

Remember the leader's job is to ask the questions. Let others do the answering. Your work as the leader is to help the group to *discover for themselves* what the Bible says. If there is hesitancy in answering, remember that a few moments of silence won't hurt. You may repeat or reword any questions. Give people time to think!

The person leading the sample study should simply read the questions. Read them in such a way that others will be encouraged to take a turn being the discussion leader.

SAMPLE STUDY:

First, pass out Bibles with bookmarks placed at Mark 2:1 so that no one will have difficulty finding the place. Then, ask someone to read aloud Mark 2:1-12. Next, move through the paragraph by discussing the following questions:

1. Where and why does the crowd gather?

2. What indications of Jesus' popularity are there at this time?

3. Why and how is Jesus' preaching interrupted? What is his reaction to this interruption?

4. What, do you think, do the paralytic's friends have in mind? Compare with what Jesus says in verse 5.

5. Who reacts to this statement? How? Why? Look up "scribes" and "blasphemy" in a collegiate dictionary. Under Jewish law, blasphemy was punishable by death.

6. In your own words what are the scribes saying? How does Jesus answer? What is the point of Jesus' question in verse 9?

7. What does Jesus expect to prove to the scribes by healing the paralyzed man?

8. How does the paralytic express his faith? What are the reactions to his healing? With whom do the people connect the healing?

Now, sum up briefly what you have discovered together from this study.

Conclude the study of Mark 2:1-12 by suggesting some applications:

The paralyzed man needed his four friends to help bring him to Jesus. However, the man himself eventually had to respond in faith to Jesus' command. His friends could not help him then.

In this incident Jesus stated his authority (the right and the power) to forgive sins. How do you react to his claim?

Do you know someone in need? You may have the opportunity to act as the paralytic's friends did. As in Mark 2, it may cost you time and energy, and the exercise of faith.

NEXT, distribute copies of the study guide *Mark: Examine the Record*. Ask everyone to turn to the questions on Mark 2:1-12. Point out that these questions were the ones you asked in leading the study in which they have just participated. Suggest that with these questions anyone in the group could have led the group to discover the main emphasis of the paragraph.

Suggest that a good leader will take time in preparation to study the chapter thoroughly, then to go over the questions several times so that he/she can guide the group smoothly through the study.

CLOSE YOUR PRESENTATION
BY ASKING:

"Are you interested in trying this kind of discussion group?" Begin with those who are interested. Any number from four to eight makes a good start for a discussion group. If you have twelve or more people each week, divide and form two groups. Others will soon join the smaller groups.

PLAN AHEAD:

At the introductory meeting, set a day and a time to meet the following week. Get a volunteer to host the gathering. You or someone else plan to be the question-asker for the study of the first chapter of Mark. Urge everyone to read chapter one of Mark's Gospel during the week.

Make sure everyone has a copy of the study guide *Mark: Examine the Record*. Suggest that each person read the introductory section, "How to Use This Study Guide," as well as going over the questions for the first chapter during the week. If everyone does not have a guide, time is wasted as the discussion leader has to keep repeating questions.

Groups should grow and divide. If a group is too large, a few individuals will dominate and quieter persons won't participate. A group of 8–12 is ideal for discussion and for sharing leadership.

Baby sitting is often a necessity. If possible, have the children cared for in a different home to avoid distraction.

AND SO BEGIN . . . THAT'S HOW!

MORE ADVICE FOR HOSTS AND DISCUSSION LEADERS:

Arrange chairs so that each person can see all the others in the group. Some groups may wish to sit around a table. Serve any refreshments as people arrive. Don't wait until everyone is there. At the time agreed upon, interrupt the flow of conversation and begin the study.

A Small Group Bible Study is not a prayer group. However, the leader for the day should begin with a brief prayer asking God's wisdom and direction in the Bible study. The prayer may be written or extemporaneous. Or the leader may *ask* someone else to pray, but this must be done *beforehand*, not on the spur of the moment. Praying aloud before a group can be frightening to anyone who is doing it for the first time.

Next, read the Bible section for the day aloud before discussing it. Assign the reading by paragraphs or other larger units, rather than by single verses.

The Gospel of Mark is recommended as the first unit of study. Mark is the shortest of the four Gospels and the study may be completed in four months. In order to understand the Gospel of Mark you don't need background in other books of the Bible.

The study guide provides questions to help the leader guide the group through the chapter. *Use the questions in your own study preparation.* Think through the possible answers to the questions until you are familiar with the Bible portion to be discussed. At the discussion ask the questions given in the guide.

If the group, in answering a question, answers another question before it is asked, *skip the already answered question and go on to the next one.* It is not necessary to go rigidly through the study using each question. You are studying the Bible, not the study guide! The more familiar you are with the study passage and questions, the more flexible you can be in leading the discussion.

17

If someone answering misses the point of a question or gives only part of the answer, say: "What do some of the rest of you think?" or, "Is there more to this?"

Receive contributions to the discussion with a positive attitude, but don't evaluate by saying, "Yes, that is true" or "No, that is wrong." If someone has misread the passage, ask, "Is that really what this says?"

As a discussion goes on, if the same people seem to do all the talking, preface your next thought question with, "Don't answer this question immediately, but think about it. The question is. . . ." Allow a minute or two of silence. Then repeat the question and call by name one of the people who has not spoken much in the discussion. Often a

quiet person indicates by facial expression that he has something to say, and he will say it if encouraged to do so.

Encourage people to share specific illustrations of how the passage under study applies in their lives. If the study reveals failures or shortcomings in your own life, be honest enough to admit this. If you are honest in sharing your own needs, others will be more likely to be so.

Be sure you don't talk too much as the leader. Try to redirect those questions which are asked you. A discussion should move back and forth among members. It should not be simply a question and answer session between the leader on one side and the group members on the other.

During the first few sessions when a group tends to be rather quiet, the leader will have to stimulate discussion by asking and re-asking questions and encouraging members to speak out.

Once a warm sense of fellowship is established in a group and everyone feels free to communicate his or her ideas on the chapter, the job of leader becomes that of a moderator. The leader should start the group discussion on time, try to keep it moving ahead on the main points, and bring the study to a conclusion in the time allotted to the group.

To guide a group through the designated portion of Scripture within a limited time requires that each leader make decisions about the relative value of the different lines of thought which arise in a discussion. Some questions will have to be handled briefly for more important ones to be adequately discussed.

In preparing a study, pray for ability to guide the discussion with love and understanding. In your

mind or on paper, divide the available discussion time into sections, allotting appropriate amounts of time to different parts of the study passage. Once you get into the discussion, be flexible, but try to keep within the general time limits you have set for each section of the study. Don't let the group discuss the first paragraph of a chapter at such length that only one-quarter of the time remains to study three-quarters of the chapter.

Allow a few minutes at the end of the discussion to summarize the impact which the study portion has upon life today. The discussion leader or a group member may summarize.

INDUCTIVE BIBLE STUDY

The Bible is a collection of books. Each book should be studied to discover its own message before you approach the Bible topically. Guides in the Small Group Bible Studies series help you to study each book using the inductive method.

To *approach the Bible inductively* is to read it thoughtfully (as you would read a book, a newspaper, or a letter) to discover what it says, what it means, and what application it has to your life.

The inductive questions in the study guides enable the thoughtful person to study the source-book of Christianity and to find out what the Christian message is.

A Small Group Bible Study discussion gives time and opportunity for a high degree of learning, providing an informal atmosphere which promotes openness in sharing. People ask questions they have previously thought were too stupid or insignificant to raise in a large group or to ask their minister or priest. Often these questions are profound and hit at basic spiritual issues.

THE FORMAT OF STUDY GUIDES

A noted educator says about questions: "All our knowledge results from questions; question asking is our most important intellectual tool." He points out that a badly formed question produces no knowledge and no understanding. Skillfully formed, a question leads to new facts, new perspectives, new ideas.

Study guides contain many questions to stimulate you to think, and to make fresh discoveries in the Bible. Fill-in spaces for answers are not provided since they tend to direct or limit the amount of thinking you will do on a verse or paragraph.

The format of the study guides promotes an atmosphere of spontaneity. New learning takes place during the group discussion. This does not happen if people are reading their prepared answers to one another. Advance preparation is important, however. If members of your group prepare well, you will move more quickly and at greater depth during the discussion.

You may use your study guide again with another group. The same book of the Bible studied at a later time with different people will reveal new treasures.

RECOMMENDED ORDER OF STUDY to build a framework of Bible knowledge:

Gospel of Mark		Gospel of Mark
Acts		Acts
Gospel of John	OR	Four Men of God
and/or		Romans
Romans		and/or
Four Men of God		Gospel of John

Then you may wish to alternate New Testament Gospels and Epistles with Old Testament studies.

Think creatively! START A BIBLE STUDY DISCUSSION GROUP at home, at work, or in your community with:

Couples in the neighborhood
Business or professional colleagues
Mothers with pre-schoolers
PTA members
Men's breakfast group
Career singles
Recently widowed or divorced people
Young marrieds
Members of your residents association
Fellow workers or students at lunch hour
Military families or singles
Members of your labor union
High school or college age students
New members of your church
Tennis group or bowling team
Newcomers
Foster parents
Senior citizens
Nursery school mothers
Nursing home residents
Prisoners in jails

STUDIES IN THIS SERIES

Available from Marshall Morgan & Scott

How to Start a Small Group Bible Study A Guide to
Discussion Study

Mark: Examine the Record (recommended as first unit of
study)

The Acts of the Apostles

Romans

Four Men of God Abraham, Joseph, Moses, David